THE LINN COUNTY FAMILY OUTDOOR GUIDE

EVERYTHING YOU NEED TO ENJOY NATURE LOCALLY

BY BRIANNA BARANOWSKI

ISBN: 979-8-218-38441-8

This book is dedicated to my boys, who make life a grand adventure every single day.

TABLE OF CONTENTS

INTRODUCTION

Although I would have considered myself an outdoor enthusiast from childhood, I didn't really embrace nature as a *mom* until the COVID pandemic first hit in 2020. With two boys under three and nowhere to 'go,' well, we went. Outside. And while daily walks around the neighborhood were nice (and the dog sure loved them), I can't say they brought me much joy. I found myself wanting more. In fact, I *needed* more. I felt trapped inside our insular bubble.

And so we took our walks beyond the suburbs. Like so many other families, we wandered to the woods. There was a definitive shift in our family dynamics. Instead of the pressure to constantly entertain and protect our children, my husband and I were able to step back and observe their inquisitive and imaginative minds at work. We'd never get very far on any trail, but we could spend hours just being present. Just, *breathing.* Just, genuinely enjoying each other's company.

We slowly dabbled in local explorations. As you'll read later on, Pinicon Ridge was (and remains) a favorite of ours. But at that point in 2020, we stuck to fair weather conditions. That tendency to stay inside during colder months was mostly because of me. Growing up in Southern California, I hadn't learned yet to 'warm up' to the idea of Iowa winters beyond the novelty Christmas aspect of it all.

Fast forward to the end of 2022. I noticed a few online friends celebrating 1,000 hours spent outside. I was intrigued! I read a little more about this #1000hoursoutside challenge and learned about the devastating effects of nature deprivation that kids are currently encountering. After reading that American children spend an average of ten minutes outside a day, compared to the average seven hours a day they spend in front of a screen, I felt the winds of change blow right through me.

I'll be honest, the 2021-2022 winter had been especially hard for me personally; by that spring I absolutely hated living here. In fact, Mother's Day 2022 will forever be etched in my memory. After a dreadfully dreary early spring, I thought I needed a warm and sunny Mother's Day to turn things around. And when the gray sky loomed and the drizzle refused to dissipate, I broke down. It was like all nine years of living in Iowa smacked me in the heart at once. I could no longer handle the 'bad' weather. I cried and begged my husband to find a way for us to move back to California. I let years of resentment and unmet expectations pour out of me like the rain assaulting the kitchen windows.

It wasn't my finest moment. But I'm glad it happened. Because after hearing me out, my husband asked me to give Iowa one more year. And with it, to embrace the weather for what it is, not what I expected it to be.

So when I saw those #1000hoursoutside posts December 2022, I knew what we needed to do. We decided to commit to the challenge and embrace being outside throughout the entire next year. We bundled up on January 1st and wandered around Wanatee Park. Sure, it was only for an hour, but that was an hour longer than we'd typically spend outside that time of year.

Slowly but surely, we branched out and tried as many local areas we could find. And you know what we discovered? That Linn County, Iowa is absolutely GORGEOUS. Its beauty is not bound to the clear summer skies or the crisp kaleidoscope of leaves changing in the fall. We found countless ways to appreciate where we live in the quiet stillness of winter and the bursting slingshot of life in the drizzly spring.

Who knew? Certainly not me. Without traveling more than thirty minutes, we found nature's playground time and time again.

I'd like to say the rest is history, but it's more like an ongoing journey that's very much a part of our family's present. We ended 2023 with 1,028 hours outside. And I can't guarantee we'll always love going on these adventures together, but I sure hope we do. And even if in 5 or 10 years the boys have become too busy or disinterested in little nature outings with their parents, we'll still always have these core memories of the phase of life our little family shifted the way we spend our time together. We'll look back fondly on the thousands of hours as young, wild boys and two awe-inspired parents. I'll look through the photos, or pick up a special rock or mussel shell one of the boys gifted me when he was young and full of wonder, and I'll smile. I'll have no regrets.

And neither will you. Whether you're looking to hit 1,000 or 10 hours outside in the year, I hope your time is filled with beauty and wonder. I hope that this book takes you to new places, or gives a familiar place fresh eyes. I hope your family creates beautiful memories together. But also, as the adult reading this, I hope you're able to invite your inner child along to embrace all the glory and sense of wonder Linn County has to offer.

HOW THIS BOOK IS ORGANIZED

There are so many wonderful places to enjoy nature in Linn County, it certainly made it difficult to narrow down which places to feature for this guide! For the sake of clear organization, I *mostly* stuck with places highlighted on Linn County Conservation's website (https://www.linncountyiowa.gov/conservation). These are grouped by:

Iowa State Parks within Linn County
Linn County Parks
Linn County Trails (with three extra trails included)
Linn County Preserves
Natural Areas in Linn County
Extra Places Worth Noting (in my humble opinion)

Now what's the difference between a park, a preserve, and a natural area? I'm glad you asked! I certainly didn't know either, until I spoke with Meredith Glynn, Office Coordinator at Linn County Conservation. As explained by Meredith,

"Each area has its own specific rules and regulations and there are some exceptions to the general natural area/ preserve name. For example, some hunting areas have trails, and some preserves allow hunting of specific wildlife, but I will try to hit on the basic differences.

Natural areas are wild spaces (typically little to no trails or amenities) designated for hunting activities.

Preserves do not allow hunting and often have minimal trails, and some have primitive amenities (such as pit vault style restrooms).

Parks are developed spaces with many trails and modern amenities like water, electricity, playgrounds, and paved roadways/trails."

Because of this, and from my field research exploring these areas, you might notice more space dedicated to the parks, trails, and preserves than the natural areas. With the exception of the Matsell Bridge, I will focus more on the facts of these natural areas. And if your family enjoys hunting, I've included the specific requirements and hunting regulations for the various natural areas as well.

When reading this guide, you can start from the beginning or skip around for inspiration. There are seasonal and locally-minded bucket lists to check off, a section of recommendations based on various specific interests you may have, and journaling components for your own reflection. Feel free to mark it up! I also personally think this guide would be a fun gift for someone who just moved to the area, or even as a 'hand me down' to a friend once you've completed everything. Sure, it wouldn't be as great for my book sales to encourage you to share this book instead of buying new, but how fun for a friend or neighbor to follow your well traveled footsteps and add on to your notes! What a wealth of knowledge you could build.

However you choose to use this book, I hope your inner naturalist shines through. May you grow in your plant identifying abilities, have an exciting encounter with an animal while on the trail, and tap into that sense of wonder you might have silenced in adulthood. Enjoy.

PLANNING AND PACKING

1. Dress appropriately for the weather. I know, duh, but it has to be said. No matter the season, wearing the right clothes will make a huge difference in how long you last outside. You don't need cute or designer clothes to play in nature, but you DO need a good winter coat and gloves for the winter, and breathable fabric for summer.
2. If your budget allows, find a pair of sturdy shoes or hiking boots that can be reserved for your adventures so the rest of your footwear stays in decent shape.
3. Pack enough food to feed an army. Just kidding, sort of. But nothing melts down a trip quicker than hangry little ones. We like to pack an easy lunch for a picnic but also make sure to include plenty of desirable snacks for everybody. I'm also not above packing a couple of surprise sweets for extra motivation.
4. Bug spray, bug spray, bug spray. Unless it's winter. During winter months you can enjoy a bug-free existence outside. It's glorious.
5. If exploring in the winter months, make sure the park is open and accessible to the public beforehand.
6. If your kids are reluctant to get out and explore, consider making it a fun challenge. We track our hours outside with the #1000hoursoutside app (and celebrate with ice cream every 100 hours), but some families prefer to track miles walked or places explored. This book includes a few checklists you can follow as a family. Whatever you decide, discuss it as a family for more buy-in.
7. Find the time of day that works best for *your* family. Every family has a different set of priorities, preferences, and schedules. For this particular season of our lives, we like to get out of the house a little after morning snack (9:30ish)

and try to get home by what used to be the end of rest time (1:30-2:00). This means lunch and an afternoon snack outside and typically a short nap on the drive home. Because of our work and school schedules, we stick to weekends when it isn't summer. Truth be told, I'd love to get more after school/evening outings under our belts, but the kids are usually wiped out after school and I want to respect their need to relax at home.

WHAT'S IN OUR BACKPACK?

NOTE: I also like to carry a small fanny pack for more easily accessible items: my phone, a small sunscreen stick, and an extra front pocket for small treasures.

Spring/Summer

- A clear zipper pouch filled with sunscreen, Bug Soother, and natural tick spray
- A filled water bottle for each of us, sometimes with a spare bottle for refills if it's extra hot
- Hats and sunglasses (prescription sunglasses were the best purchase I made in 2023. Who knew you could see leaves so crisply?!)
- Bug cage and nets
- Lunch and snacks in a separate bag with ice packs
- A small bag for 'treasures' if we're allowed to bring things home: feathers, bones, shells, fossils, etc. Check with each place before taking anything.
- If foraging, a mesh bag and small knife or pruning shears (optional)

- Phone for GPS and photo purposes

Fall/Winter

- Binoculars for bird watching
- Lunch bag with all our food (depending on weather, ice pack optional)
- Extra gloves and hats for kids in case theirs get too wet
- A small bag for 'treasures' if we're allowed to bring things home: feathers, bones, shells, fossils, etc. Check with each place before taking anything.
- Phone for GPS and photo purposes
- Make sure to have old towels and bags in the trunk for after your outing. Place wet clothes in a bag to wash later and set wet boots on the towel to protect your car. With the right snow gear, all inside layers should be dry and warm enough for inside the vehicle.

A NOTE REGARDING CARRY IN, CARRY OUT:

You may notice signs at some of the parks asking guests to leave no trace, or to "carry in, carry out" while there. This means that the park does not have garbage cans for disposing of your trash. This is for several reasons: less maintenance, fewer animals getting into garbage, and less mess at the park.

While this may seem inconvenient at first, I promise that with a bit of planning you won't mind it at all. Just bring a used grocery bag with you, or have food storage that you can keep wrappers in after eating. And then when you're home, you can dispose of the trash!

IOWA STATE PARKS

PLEASANT CREEK

PALISADES-KEPLER

WAPSIPINICON

PLEASANT CREEK STATE PARK

4530 McClintock Road
Palo, IA 52324
https://www.iowadnr.gov/Places-to-Go/State-Parks/Iowa-
State-Parks/Pleasant-Creek-State-Recreation-Area

Pleasant Creek brings the beach scene to Iowa! I love this park primarily because of the lake and beach. It's never *super* crowded, parking is easy, and the water has been ideal for teaching my boys how to swim. They love to practice going underwater and floating while at the beach! You can bring your inflatable paddle board or kayak behind the ropes and do quick little paddles with the kids. On the rare occasion you find yourself at the beach alone, you can sunbathe on your paddle board while hooking your toe around the rope. That way you don't float away while relaxing!

Another lovely feature of this park is its campgrounds. They're clean, scenic, and close to plenty of recreational options.

And don't discount this place over the winter! The multi-use trail is perfect for cross country skiing and snowmobiling. We also love to build snow forts and snowmen along the water, and cross the frozen lake while admiring the ice fishing tents plopped all around. While I haven't personally ice fished here, it seems to be a popular spot in the wintertime.

Months of Operation: Park is open year round, see below for additional camping information.

Pet Information: Domestic pets allowed throughout park and camping/cabin accommodations. Trails are horseback friendly.

Playground: There is an older, metal playground near the campground and fairly close to the beach area.

Lodging: There are three campgrounds and four rustic cabins available to reserve seasonally (typically April 15-October 15). The campgrounds have nice bathrooms and showers. It should be noted that the campgrounds are non-equestrian. When our family camped here, we found the views scenic and loved being surrounded by native restored prairie. You can walk to the beach from the first campground, though I recommend a wagon for all your beach gear!

Trails: Something unique about Pleasant Creek is its interpretive trail. It's a short, one mile hike. The multi-use trail is eight miles. Both trails are loops and considered 'moderate' in difficulty. We found that in June, the swamp area on the interpretive trail was full of mosquitoes. I was covered in bites by the end of that short hike!

Stroller/ Accessibility: Neither trails are stroller or wheelchair accessible. The park manager, Matt Bonar, described them as "fairly rough." There is a paved path from the beach parking lot to the sand. However, it is steep.

Bathroom Situation: There are three non-modern year-round restrooms, and seven seasonal modern restrooms. The beach restrooms also have outdoor rinsing areas to get all that sand off. But good luck keeping those kids' feet sand-free between the showers and the car! That's just impossible no matter where you go.

Other features: The lake and designated beach area are what sets Pleasant Creek apart from other Linn County destinations. The lake is 410 acres and a no-wake body of water. This means that Pleasant Creek is popular for fishing, kayaking, paddleboarding, windsurfing, pontoon boating, and scuba diving. The beach has a marked off area for open water swimming and inflatable fun. Just remember that life jackets are always required beyond the open water swimming area!

Whether from a small boat or the rocky shoreline, fishing is a must here at Pleasant Creek. The water is well stocked and fairly clear. Come visit in the winter and you'll see plenty of ice fishing happening on the lake! There is a fish cleaning station available for use.

There are also 1,517 acres of public hunting ground and a field dog trial space.

Must See or Do: Spend a day at the beach, make s'mores by the campfire, safely cross the frozen lake and check for animal tracks on the ice.

NOTES:

Date Visited:	
Special Memory:	
Something We'd Like to Do Next Time:	

PALISADES-KEPLER STATE PARK

700 Kepler Dr
Mount Vernon, IA 52314
https://www.iowadnr.gov/Places-to-Go/State-Parks/Iowa-
State-Parks/Palisades-Kepler-State-Park

Palisades-Kepler is a gorgeous park nestled off Highway 30 in Mount Vernon. Popular for its day use trails and Cedar River bluff views, this is one your family of all ages will enjoy.

Some of the best spring ephemeral wildflowers I've encountered have been at Palisades-Kepler (just off the Lodge Trail). My boys like exploring the sandy river bank: looking for opalescent mussel shells, building with driftwood, and keeping a keen eye out for eagles.

There's a wide variety of trail types and overlooks, as well as a boat ramp and overnight accommodations. For the hobby hiker, I recommend the Cedar Cliff trail. It's challenging, but kids can handle it. The views cannot be beat, and the geological sightings are enough to bring in several college course field trips throughout the year.

Months of Operation: Palisades-Kepler is open year round, though it should be noted that this park does not have a storm shelter for extreme weather conditions.

Pet Information: Dogs allowed and must be on a leash. My puppy loved exploring the trails at Palisades.

Playground: There is no playground. Let nature be your playground when you're here.

Lodging: There are 45 campsites, four family cabins, and two shelters available for reservations. Something unique about Palisades-Kepler is its youth group campsite available for larger groups. Camping and shelters can be reserved or available by walk-up year-round. Their limestone lodge is a beautiful building rich in history. Almost one hundred years old, it would make a great place for a special occasion.

When not reserved, the open air shelters are the perfect spot for an impromptu picnic.Their cabins are seasonally available April 1st-October 15th.

Trails: There are six trails that are all two miles long or less, though they range in difficulty from easy (Overlook) to hard (Campers, Cedar Cliff, Cool Hollow, Lodge). They offer beautiful views and a diverse setting of geological features, river bluffs, a variety of trees and plants, and animals. When hiking in October, we noticed so many chipmunks preparing for the winter ahead! I personally prefer this park in the spring and fall; there are unique finds here during those seasons and far fewer bugs. If you visit in the summer, make sure to pack your bug spray!

Stroller/ Accessibility: The trails are not stroller or wheelchair accessible, though the park manager did share that he sees many hikers taking the paved roads for their own hiking purposes. If you choose to walk the roads, please be mindful of vehicles.

Bathroom Situation: There are several modern restrooms available seasonally, and one non-modern restroom open year-round.

Other features: This park has ample picnic areas spread throughout the park for families to enjoy a snack or meal together outside. There are also fishing spots, overlooks, rock climbing (you must check in with the park office to register before climbing), and sandy riverbanks. Keep in mind that although swimming in the Cedar River is allowed, it can be dangerous. Personally, we never swim rivers; the currents are too strong.

Must See or Do: Take a family walk along the Cedar River in the fall after the leaves have begun to change, go for a wildflower walk in early spring, host a large picnic with friends and family.

NOTES:

Date Visited:	
Special Memory:	
Something We'd Like to Do Next Time:	

WAPSIPINICON STATE PARK

21301 County Road E34
Anamosa, IA 52205

https://www.iowadnr.gov/Places-to-Go/State-Parks/Iowa-State-Parks/Wapsipinicon-State-Park

Often considered "Iowa's best kept secret," Wapsipinicon State Park is worth letting the cat out of the bag! One morning, I saw a friend post on Facebook about her kids' creek stompin' afternoon. I took one look at those pictures and immediately texted her, "Okay, WHERE is that?!" I knew my boys would love to visit a place like that, and I was right! So thanks, Melissa, you shared this gem with us and we've been visiting often ever since. This almost 400 acre park has trails, camping, golfing, caves, historic bridges, and the beautiful Wapsi River flowing through it.

Located in Anamosa, I highly recommend a visit to Wapsipinicon. Pack a lunch, a few nets, and some sunscreen and spend the afternoon exploring Dutch Creek. Stand on the side of the upside down bridge near the creek and encourage cars to drive past and splash you. Catch a crayfish or two. And when the heat is getting to be too much, head a short distance to the ice cave for a nice cool down.

Months of Operation: This park is open year-round, with plenty to do during the winter months.

Pet Information: While there is not a designated pet area or dog park, pets are allowed on a leash at Wapsipinicon State Park. I know we've seen plenty of pups cooling off at Dutch Creek! Dogs are not allowed on the golf course.

Playground: There is one playground. It has swings, slides, and climbing areas. A perk of this playground is its proximity to the creek, upside down bridge, and picnic shelters.

Lodging: The campground at Wapsipinicon offers many shaded campsites. Half of the sites have electrical hook ups. There are two day-use lodges, the Boy Scout Lodge and Rotary Lodge. You can reserve these online. There are also open air shelters available for online reservations. The shelters are located near the playground and Dutch Creek.

Trails: There are many short trails to explore here! A whopping fifteen trails wind through the park, many connecting with one another. They range from easy to hard and individually are all less than a mile. Ten of the fifteen trails are multi-use and suitable for cross country skiing and snowmobiling in the winter.

Stroller/ Accessibility: The Hale Bridge Trail is the only paved trail, though many visitors of this park walk along the side of the road for smoother surface access. The other trails are either mowed grass, dirt, or crushed rock.

Bathroom Situation: While there are four restroom buildings at Wapsipinicon State Park, only one of them is open year-round (located near the Boy Scout Lodge). The other restrooms are open seasonally.

Other features: Wapsipinicon boasts many unique gems that set it apart from other parks. For one, it has a nine-hole golf course and clubhouse. For golfing information, call: (319) 462-3930. It also has two caves: Ice Cave and Horse Thief Cave. The caves are the perfect way to beat the heat during summer!

Must See or Do: Walk the Hale Bridge, the last three-strand bowstring arch bridge in Iowa. This bridge is why Wapsipinicon

State Park is on the National Register of Historic Places. It provides a gorgeous view of the Wapsi River, and is a short walk to take with little kids. A trip to Wapsipinicon State Park would not be complete without a float on the river or some good old fashioned creek stomping at Dutch Creek!

NOTES:

Date Visited:	
Special Memory:	
Something We'd Like to Do Next Time:	

LINN COUNTY PARKS

BUFFALO CREEK

MORGAN CREEK

PINICON RIDGE

WANATEE

BUFFALO CREEK PARK

1825 Coggon Road, Coggon, IA 52218
https://www.linncountyiowa.gov/963/Buffalo-Creek-Park

Did you know that Buffalo Creek Park was the first park developed in Linn County? Much of the park was developed in the 1960s, with exciting new accommodations and improvements completed in 2023. The creek is bustling with activity; I'll never forget scouting this park and finding a runaway cow climbing down to the creek for a few sips of frigid water. This cow seemed completely unbothered by its distance from the ranch it came from.

I predict that Buffalo Creek will be a hit among Linn County residents now that is boasts a brand new playground and improved campgrounds. The park has wetlands, the creek, and plenty of woodland areas to explore. It's recommended to visit in the spring for its impressive array of wildflowers.

Months of Operation: Buffalo Creek Park is open daily like other parks (4:30AM-10:30PM), however, the roads are closed to vehicles seasonally late October- approximately April 15th. The concrete dates depend on the ground and stream conditions.

Pet Information: There is an off-leash area near the north side of the original campground.

Playground: The new playground was completed in 2023. This new addition is located on the south end of the park. It's geared for ages 5-12 and has many climbing opportunities. The playground is divided into two areas, with one being more fit for younger kids and the other having more challenging equipment. There are only two swings.

Lodging: There are now 31 campsites located at the park. Some require a reservation, and others are first come, first served. They have electrical and water hook-ups.

There is now an open air shelter, Buffalo Creek Shelter, available for reservations.

Trails: There are two trails at Buffalo Creek. One is 1.2 miles and located at the north end of the park. It parallels the creek, as well as a few wetlands. It should be noted that the off-leash dog area is also near this trail. Something to be mindful of if your family is weary of unfamiliar dogs.

There is also a short, mowed grass trail alongside the new campground.

Stroller/ Accessibility: The north trail is level terrain with gravel surfacing. This can be bumpy, but accessible. The south trail is mowed grass but fairly flat and accessible.

Bathroom Situation: Aside from the campground amenities, there is a vault-toilet restroom near the new playground and shelter.

Other features: Buffalo Creek has one of the largest blue bell populations in the area. It also has a natural area nearby for hunting or exploring.

Must See or Do: Visit the blue bells in late April, spend the night at a campsite, enjoy the new playground amenities.

NOTES:

Date Visited:	
Special Memory:	
Something We'd Like to Do Next Time:	

MORGAN CREEK PARK

7212 E Ave NW Cedar Rapids, IA 52405
https://www.linncountyiowa.gov/964/Morgan-Creek-Park

Morgan Creek Park is a beautiful place to take your family any time of the year. While the new playground and south side entrance is quite a crowd pleaser, don't limit your time here to just that area. Sure, the playground is spectacular and the new Morgan Creek Shelter is the perfect outdoor space for your next party, but the north side is just as worthy of your time and attention.

Located within Cedar Rapids and bordering Palo, this 352-acre park has prairie, a wooded area, a creek, an arboretum, campground, and miles of accessible trails.

Months of Operation: Morgan Creek Park is open year-round.

Pet Information: There is an area near the south entrance where people can unleash their dogs for some exercise on 40 acres of land. Otherwise, pet owners must keep dogs leashed in all other areas.

It's worth noting that dogs are not allowed on the playground equipment or playground surfaces. The restrooms near the playground, however, have a really neat drinking fountain 'dog bowl' for your four-legged friends.

Playground: The playground at Morgan Creek has quickly become a local favorite for good reason. Designed with ages 5-12 in mind, this playground can easily still delight the youngest of teetering toddlers and even teens looking to grasp onto the edges of childhood. There are incredibly tall structures for climbing and sliding, many spinning options, ziplines, unique swings, and a scaffolded approach to the levels of difficulty varying from smaller structures to downright thrilling.

Lodging: There is a smaller campground on the north entrance of Morgan Creek Park. There are 35 campsites, three with electrical hook-ups. The sites are nestled behind the cover of large trees. There are no cabins. Morgan Creek has one shelter available for reservations. The Morgan Creek Shelter is located near the playground on the south side. It's a beautiful shelter that can host up to 125 people. The shelter has several tables, a grill, and a bonfire area in the back.

For picnics, there are several tables and shaded spots available near the playground.

Trails: There are several loops and longer trails at Morgan Creek. The Morgan Creek Trail (to be later described in more detail in the 'County Trails' section of this book) is in development to connect to Xavier High School and Rock Island Preserve.

Stroller/ Accessibility: The arboretum side is crushed limestone. Many of the loops near the playground are mowed grass, and would be stroller or wheelchair accessible much of the year. The Morgan Creek Trail is fully paved.

Bathroom Situation: There are seasonal and year-round restrooms at Morgan Creek Park. There is one located near the trailhead of the south entrance, two near the playground, and a few scattered near the campground.

Other features: Morgan Creek has 4.8 miles of cross country skiing trails. The arboretum and butterfly garden is unique and scenic, as well as the creek from where the park received its name.

Must See or Do: Join in with the kids and have fun on the playground (I personally recommend the zipline), go biking or scootering on the Morgan Creek Trail, take a walk to the butterfly garden.

NOTES:

Date Visited:	
Special Memory:	
Something We'd Like to Do Next Time:	

PINICON RIDGE PARK

4729 Horseshoe Falls Road
Central City, IA 52214
https://www.mycountyparks.com/county/linn/park/
pinicon-ridge-park.aspx

Pinicon Ridge Park holds a special place in our hearts. It's where we first started to explore Linn County more seriously during the very beginnings of COVID. It seems that every time we visit this park, we find ourselves having yet another 'awe-inspired' moment. The trails are gorgeous, the playgrounds are unique and updated, there's plenty of wildlife (this is one of the 'buggier' areas in my experience), and there are spaces for kids to roam and explore. It's a multi-season favorite for sure!

Months of Operation: Park is open year round, lodging is seasonal.

Pet Information: Yes, dogs are allowed but must be leashed on trails and near the playgrounds. There is a dog exercise area near the water concession stand. It should be noted that pets are not allowed in the cabins.

Playground: There are two playgrounds, one is near the Woodpecker trail and the other is in the campground area. Both of these playgrounds are challenging, engaging, and blend in aesthetically with the natural landscape surrounding them.

Lodging: There is a campground for tent or RV camping, group campsite spots, and four cabins available to rent. Season for lodging is generally April 15th-October 15th. Cabins must be reserved online, but camping is first come, first served.

There are also two enclosed lodges (Horseshoe Falls and Woodpecker) available year-round and four open air shelters (Eagle View, Flying Squirrel, Riverside, and Wapsi Bluff) available for reservations April 15th-October 15th.

Trails: There are four trails: Flying Squirrel, White Oak, Woodpecker Hill, and the Wapsi-River Trail.

The Woodpecker Hill is the shortest, at 1.7 miles. It takes an estimated 45 minutes to walk. Although this trail has some hills, toddlers are able to hike it with supervision. About halfway through the trail is "Horseshoe Falls," a small water cascade that's fun to explore with littles.

Stroller/ Accessibility: The Wapsi-River Trail is hard surface, as well as the paths around the playground and Mary Lundby Bridge.

Bathroom Situation: There are a few seasonal restrooms throughout the park, with individual doors that lock. They are located in the campground, near the playground, and in the Wapsi Bluff Shelter. There are also primitive, year-round restrooms along the entrance road.

Other features: Hunting (only in designated areas near the North entrance), fishing, lit sledding hill, water concession rentals (with a shuttle service for tubing and floating), the Alexander Wildlife Area (with elk nearby), observation tower.

Must See or Do: Go frog catching, climb the observation tower, cross the Mary Lundby Bridge at night, have a picnic at the Wapsi Bluff Shelter (if it's not already reserved).

NOTES:

Date Visited:	
Special Memory:	
Something We'd Like to Do Next Time:	

WANATEE PARK

1600 Banner Drive Marion, IA 52302
https://www.linncountyiowa.gov/966/Wanatee-Park

Wanatee (formerly named Squaw Creek) Park is a local favorite here in Marion. We first started visiting Wanatee primarily for the lively dog park scene. K-9 Acres is busy, popular, and well maintained. Our love for Wanatee only grew as we explored further!

The campgrounds are ideally located and the restrooms near them are exceptional. While we've enjoyed the trails, it should be noted that we've been lost more than once. I recommend bringing a map of the park with you while you hike.

Our favorite thing to do at Wanatee these days is visit the campground playground. It's beautiful, never crowded, and there's a forager's wealth of edible plants all along the perimeter (mulberries, sumac, grapes). But be warned-there's also plenty of poison ivy near the boundary as well!

In the winter, you can visit the well lit snow sports hill or try the 3.5 mile cross-country ski trail.

Months of Operation: Park is open year round, see below for additional camping and trail months of operation.

Pet Information: This park is very pet friendly. There are equestrian trails for horses, and the K-9 Acres Dog Park is located near the main entrance. There is also a small dog exercise area near the lodges. Dogs must be leashed on all other trails, and are not allowed on the campground playground.

Playground: There are two playgrounds. An older (but still super fun) playground is located near the Meadowlark Shelter. Behind the campground restrooms there is a newer, very dynamic playground designed for children five and older.

Lodging: There is tent and RV camping available approximately April 15th- October 15th. Loop A is reservation only, Loop B is first come, first served. It should be noted that Loop A is the only campground in the Linn County Parks system that allows reservations in advance. There are sheltered restrooms and showers, and two sanitary dumping stations nearby.

There are two enclosed lodges (Prairie Oak and Red Cedar) and one open air shelter available for reservations.

Trails: The Wanatee Trail is four miles long and in operation January 10th-October 1st. The trail is then closed to the public for antlerless deer bow hunting. The trail offers a nice variety of scenery, including mature trees, meadows, and creek bottoms. There are many plants and animals to observe. This trail can get pretty buggy in the summer.

There is also a popular mountain bike, equestrian, and cross-country ski trail.

Stroller/ Accessibility: The campground and adjacent newer playground is well paved, but the trails are not particularly stroller friendly.

Bathroom Situation: There are several individually locking restrooms around the park.

Other features: Hunters can apply for a limited number of licenses to bow hunt antlerless deer from October 1st- January 10th.

Must See or Do: Take a nature hike, stomp around in the snow in the winter, take your dog out to socialize without a leash at K-9 Acres.

NOTES:

Date Visited:	
Special Memory:	
Something We'd Like to Do Next Time:	

LINN COUNTY TRAILS

CEDAR VALLEY NATURE TRAIL

GRANT WOOD TRAIL

MORGAN CREEK TRAIL

OTHER NOTABLE TRAILS

PRAIRIE PARK FISHERY LOOP

SAC AND FOX TRAIL

BOYSON TRAIL

CEDAR VALLEY NATURE TRAIL

https://www.linncountyiowa.gov/967/Cedar-Valley-Nature-Trail

The Cedar Valley Nature Trail is an expansive, nature-filled experience for all. Although it spans across four counties and several cities, do not let that intimidate you. Trail users can enjoy this linear trail in any dosage they're comfortable with. People enjoy walking, biking, running, rollerblading, and scootering. In the winter, you can snowshoe, hike, or bike if conditions allow.

If parking at the Hiawatha Trailhead, you can also visit the Dave Wright Family Dog Park right along the path and give your dog a little socialization and exercise. What's nice about this dog park is that it doesn't get very crowded.

This trail does cross some busy streets. Though users of the trail have the right of way, it should be noted to be extra cautious when crossing heavy traffic. Make sure all vehicles stop before you continue, and be advised to talk to children beforehand about traffic safety and your family rules for crossing the street.

Months and Hours of Operation: The trail is open 4:00AM-10:30PM. It is open year-round, though it should be noted that there is no snow removal on this trail. Also, the County Home Road parking lot is closed during winter months.

Length of Trail: Cedar Valley Nature Trail is 52 miles long.

Level of Difficulty: Easy

Stroller/ Accessibility: From Johnson County to Urbana, this trail is hard surface paved. It's very stroller friendly.

Bathroom Situation: The Historic Center Point depot has modern restrooms open until sunset. There are also modern restrooms at the Hiawatha trailhead, and three primitive restrooms scattered.

NOTES:

Date Visited:	
How We Traveled (walk, bike, run):	
Something We'd Like to Do Next Time:	

GRANT WOOD TRAIL

https://www.linncountyiowa.gov/968/Grant-Wood-Trail

While a little disconnected due to private land ownership, the Grant Wood Trail is still a scenic and popular trail in Linn County.

If you'd like to stop before or after your trail exploration, park in Marion on either 62nd Street or at Waldo's Rock Park. You can then make an afternoon of the park: reading about the glacial erratic, picnicking at the first come, first served open air shelter, fishing, and enjoying access to a portable restroom.

In the late summer, you'll notice many foraging opportunities along this trail. Elderberry and sumac are abundant. In the fall, it's a pretty sight.

Kids will get a kick out of going through the tunnel under Highway 13, and if you have time, exploring Martin Creek just shy of 44th Street.

Months and Hours of Operation: Open year-round.

Length of Trail: According to the Linn County Trail Association, Grant Wood Trail is 8.5 miles in 3 segments in Linn County, and 3.8 miles in 2 segments in Jones County

Level of Difficulty: Easy

Stroller/ Accessibility: Some parts of this trail are crushed limestone, while other segments are paved. For the optimum accessibility, the Marion locations of the trail are paved and best for strollers and wheelchairs.

Bathroom Situation: While there are none indicated on the map of Grant Wood Trail, I did find a portable restroom near the Waldo's Rock parking area.

NOTES:

Date Visited:	
How We Traveled (walk, bike, run):	
Something We'd Like to Do Next Time:	

MORGAN CREEK TRAIL

https://www.linncountyiowa.gov/969/Morgan-Creek-Trail

Morgan Creek Trail started as a small stretch of paved trail within the boundaries of Morgan Creek Park. As plans have been approved and funding made available, it has extended far beyond the limits of the park. Already now connected to the Cherokee Trail in Cedar Rapids, walkers or bikers alike can now get from Morgan Creek to Cherry Hill Park.

The trail is also in development to extend to Xavier High School and Rock Island Preserve in Cedar Rapids.

Trail parking is located on the south entrance of Morgan Creek Park, which is also where a year-round vault toilet can be found. It's a great spot if you'd like to do a short walk before getting to the playground; long enough to help you feel accomplished, but short enough that kiddos can do it without issue (or too much complaining).

Months and Hours of Operation: This trail is open year-round. It is open for cross-country skiing, something to note if you're an enthusiast of that sport. Otherwise, it's safe to assume there is no snow removal during winter months.

Length of Trail: Less than twenty miles long.

Level of Difficulty: Easy

Stroller/ Accessibility: Morgan Creek Trail is paved and considered multi-use; it should be accessible for strollers and wheelchairs.

Bathroom Situation: There are restrooms available within Morgan Creek Park.

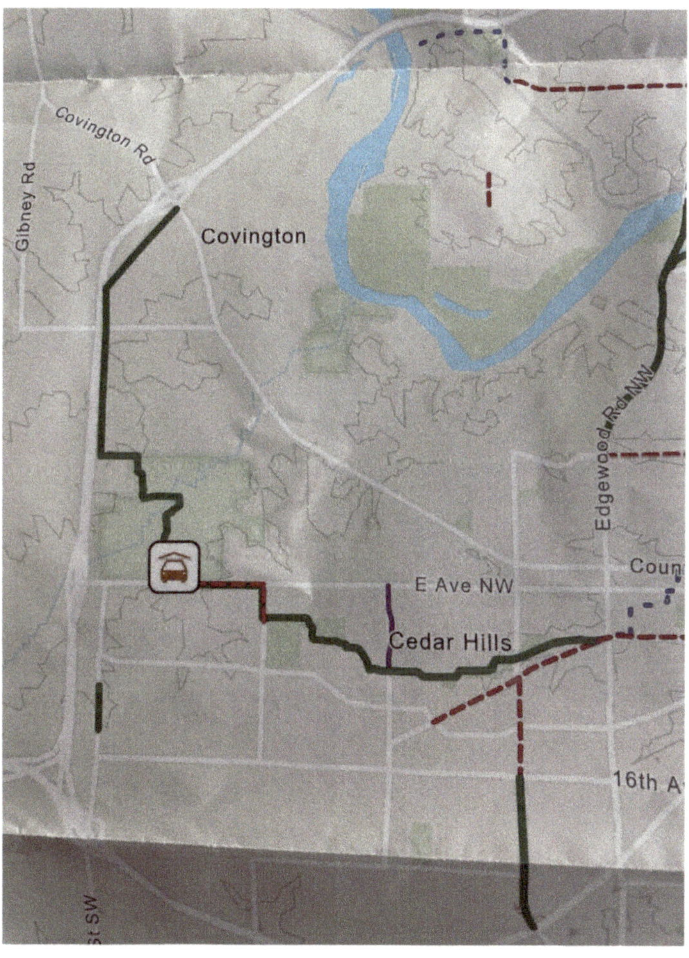

NOTES:

Date Visited:	
How We Traveled (walk, bike, run):	
Something We'd Like to Do Next Time:	

PRAIRIE PARK FISHERY LOOP

https://www.cedar-rapids.org/residents/
parks_and_recreation/recreational_trails.php

Located off Otis Road in Cedar Rapids, Prairie Park Fishery Loop is perfect for the undecided walker (or family with a wildcard child whose willingness to walk is up in the air). In theory, the trail itself is relatively easy and quick, with an estimated 33 minutes to complete the loop. This trail connects to the popular Sac and Fox Trail, giving walkers the option to extend their adventure.

Though be warned, it took my preschooler and I a little over an hour to complete the loop with him riding his scooter. This included parts of the trail with me holding both him and his scooter. Such is life!

There are several benches and picnic tables along the path. We were amazed by all the evidence of beavers (not something we'd seen before on a trail), and by all the Bald Eagles! For this reason, I'd definitely recommend visiting in late January or early February during nest-building season! It should be noted: my phone's GPS did not take me to the correct location; once you're on Otis Road, follow the physical signs to the park.

Months and Hours of Operation: This trail is open year-round.

Length of Trail: The Prairie Park Fishery Loop is 1.8 miles long.

Level of Difficulty: Easy

Stroller/ Accessibility: This trail in particular has made great strides to be as accessible as possible. Not only is the trail itself wide and smoothly paved, but the parking lot has designated parking spots for van accessibility. There is also a wheelchair accessible path to the lake for fishing.

Bathroom Situation: There are no permanent restrooms available at Prairie Park Fishery Loop. There is a wide, portable restroom in the parking lot.

NOTES:

Date Visited:	
How We Traveled (walk, bike, run):	
Something We'd Like to Do Next Time:	

SAC AND FOX TRAIL

https://www.cedar-rapids.org/residents/
parks_and_recreation/recreational_trails.php

If you're looking for full immersion into nature, the Sac and Fox Trail is the place to visit. There are several parking lots along the trail, so you can experiment with your favorite segment. Sac and Fox is beautiful, winding you along the Cedar River and Indian Creek. You'll be surrounded by forest and prairie.

Sac and Fox has single-track mountain bike trails, making it a popular spot for adventurous bikers! Equestrian use is also permitted, though it is asked that horses use shallow water crossings instead of bridges.

While you're on Sac and Fox, you'll venture into Indian Creek Nature Center. You can veer off into any of their network of trails, or stop inside the center for a rest in the bird watching room.

Months and Hours of Operation: This trail is open year-round.

Length of Trail: Sac and Fox is 7.2 miles long.

Level of Difficulty: Varying

Stroller/ Accessibility: Sac and Fox is primarily crushed limestone, so it really depends on the conditions. I'd recommend a jogging stroller, in case it gets bumpy out there.

Bathroom Situation: Although there are many parking areas along the Sac and Fox Trail, you're best using the restroom located inside the Indian Creek Nature Center.

NOTES:

Date Visited:	
How We Traveled (walk, bike, run):	
Something We'd Like to Do Next Time:	

BOYSON TRAIL

https://www.cityofmarion.org/recreation/parks-recreation/trails

Boyson Trail was one of the first trails our family ever attempted in Marion. It's one we've come back to time and time again, enchanted by the scenic views and ease of pace. Because the path is so wide, there is plenty of room for your family and other people passing by on their runs or bike rides.

The trail passes Dry Creek, which has proven to be a fun stomping area when the water levels are low enough. This is a great place to connect and try out some of Marion's parks and other trails. They've recently added more signage, helping you find your way to different hot spots in the city.

Months and Hours of Operation: This trail is open year-round. Parking on Boyson Road can get busy during summer mornings.

Length of Trail: Boyson Trail is continuously expanding and connecting with other trails, but the trail itself is 3.4 miles.

Level of Difficulty: Easy

Stroller/ Accessibility: This trail is crushed limestone, and generally accessible for strollers and wheelchairs. I've definitely gotten my stroller muddy here before! There is plenty of width on Boyson Trail for two lanes of strollers and wheelchairs.

Bathroom Situation: There is a portable restroom at the Boyson Road Trailhead, and restrooms at Thomas and Hanna Parks if you take the connections to get there.

NOTES:

Date Visited:	
How We Traveled (walk, bike, run):	
Something We'd Like to Do Next Time:	

LINN COUNTY NATURE PRESERVES

HANGING BOG

HITAGA SAND RIDGE

J. HAROLD ENNIS

MILLARD

PALISADES-DOWS

ROCK ISLAND BOTANICAL

HANGING BOG

2380 Ross Road Palo, IA 52324
https://www.linncountyiowa.gov/1118/Preserves

The Hanging Bog Preserve was donated to Linn County Conservation from the Nature Conservatory in 2023. This preserve is 15 acres and observers must follow an easement near the end of Ross Road (by the 2385 property) to access Hanging Bog without trespassing on neighboring private lands.

Because of lime deposits and a cold-water source, this unique environment allows for the rare skunk cabbage to thrive. Since skunk cabbage is one of the first blooms in late winter, I'd recommend visiting when the last snow of the season is melting for your first flower sighting of the year. It should also be noted that skunk cabbage gets its name for a reason, and the odor can be dominating.

Pay close attention as you drive down Ross Road, it's a bird watcher's dream! I couldn't believe how many woodpeckers and cardinals were flitting about while we drove.

Hours of Operation: Open year-round

Trails: Relatively easy walking at first, with some steep ravines to be mindful about. Not fully maintained, nor stroller or wheelchair friendly.

Bathroom Situation: There are no restrooms at Hanging Bog.

Must See or Do: Go birdwatching, find skunk cabbage (have kids give it a big whiff!), take a picture of an unidentified plant.

NOTES:

Date Visited:	
Special Memory:	
Something We'd Like to Do Next Time:	

HITAGA SAND RIDGE

2727 Wapsi Ridge Drive, Walker IA
https://www.linncountyiowa.gov/1118/Preserves

Hitaga Sand Ridge Prairie has some unique features that make it worth visiting. There is prickly pear cactus, a rare sight for Iowa. It is also home to the threatened (in Iowa) Ornate Box Turtle.

We liked that this preserve had high visibility in regards to the loops and winding trails. We were able to decide how long we wanted to spend there, and plan our walk accordingly.

We also loved the diverse wildlife we encountered while here!

Hours of Operation: Open year-round, sunrise to sunset.

Trails: There is a mowed path, but it can get overgrown. I would not consider this preserve stroller or wheelchair friendly. In fact, when first entering the preserve, I had to carry my four year old through the prairie section until we got to the woodland because it was so thick with thorns and burrs.

Bathroom Situation: No restrooms or toilets available.

Must See or Do: In the late summer or early fall, keep an eye out for pheasants who frequent the entrance area of this preserve. Take a walk along the 156 acres, noticing a wide variety of plants and animals. This is also a neat spot for mushroom hunting.

NOTES:

Date Visited:	
Special Memory:	
Something We'd Like to Do Next Time:	

J. HAROLD ENNIS

550 Cedar River Road Mount Vernon, IA 52314
https://www.linncountyiowa.gov/1118/Preserves

Not to be biased, but this is my personal favorite of all the nature preserves in Linn County. Clocking in at only 33 acres, this area is certainly a lesser known gem. Our Iowa Master Naturalist class visited J. Harold Ennis for a field trip on spring ephemeral woodland wildflowers. I was blown away by all the gorgeous flowers we found on our hike! Flower sightings included: spring beauty, jack-in-the-pulpit, shooting star, trillium, phlox, Dutchman's breeches, wild geranium, orchid, and more. We also found some wild ramp but I won't be sharing the exact location to protect it from over-harvesting.

There is also a well distinguished trail that takes you to the edge of the Cedar River and through lush woodlands.

Hours of Operation: Open year-round, sunrise to sunset.

Trails: There is a dirt trail that I'd consider moderate in difficulty.

Bathroom Situation: No restrooms.

Must See or Do: Visit in the spring when woodland wildflowers are at their peak (depending on the weather, check the DNR's website for specific dates each year). Find a four leaf clover. Smell the honeysuckle blossoms in the early summer (just FYI honeysuckle is an invasive species).

NOTES:

Date Visited:	
Special Memory:	
Something We'd Like to Do Next Time:	

5053 Millard Lane Central City, IA 52214
https://www.linncountyiowa.gov/1118/Preserves

Millard Preserve did not get the best first impression. Upon arrival, I questioned if I was there or not. Millard does not have a parking lot or parking spaces, so I was worried when GPS indicated I had reached my destination. I did not get out of my car that first time.

After speaking to Linn County Conservation, I discovered that I had in fact arrived at the right place. Millard, 10 acres of land donated by the Millard family, just happens to be tucked away. The second time I visited, in the late fall, the vegetation had cleared. I parked at the end of Millard Lane and found the preserve right away. Millard has a nice, short trail. I walked on a blanket of fallen oak leaves, the perfect fall accompaniment. I also happened to notice a variety of animal scat on the trail.

Hours of Operation: Millard is open year-round, sunrise to sunset.

Trails: There is a mowed trail that leads to a wetland.

Bathroom Situation: There are no restrooms.

Must See or Do: Sit on the bench near the glacial marsh and take a moment for reflection, go on a scat identification walk.

NOTES:

Date Visited:	
Special Memory:	
Something We'd Like to Do Next Time:	

PALISADES-DOWS

1365 Ivanhoe Road Mount Vernon, IA 52227
https://www.linncountyiowa.gov/1118/Preserves

If you're curious about visiting the Palisades-Dows Preserve, I highly recommend waiting until the Eastern Iowa Observatory and Learning Center is hosting an event. Run by the Cedar Amateur Astronomers, the massive observatory is certainly what makes Palisades-Dows unique and worth a visit. You can find more information about events and the Cedar Amateur Astronomers on their website: https://www.cedar-astronomers.org/.

If you happen to just show up to Palisades-Dows on a random afternoon, you might find yourself standing amongst 162-acres of beautiful land and feeling a little lost. While there is an established parking lot, there are no trails. We enjoyed all the native prairie plants blooming around the perimeter of the preserve, but the amount of poison ivy and brambles made it unsavory to walk without a trail. If you wander, wear protective clothing.

Hours of Operation: The preserve is open year-round. It should be noted that the observatory does not operate under regular hours; check the event schedule for specific operating hours.

Trails: There are no trails.

Bathroom Situation: There are restrooms inside the observatory.

Must See or Do: Attend a night of stargazing and specialized education with a local astronomer. Have a picnic on one of the many tables available.

NOTES:

Date Visited:	
Special Memory:	
Something We'd Like to Do Next Time:	

ROCK ISLAND BOTANICAL

4501 Preserve Lane Cedar Rapids, IA 52411
https://www.linncountyiowa.gov/1118/Preserves

Tucked right next to Xavier High School in Cedar Rapids, this diverse preserve is certainly worth a visit. Take a short stroll with your family or a small group of friends, and explore the rich plant species that thrive here. Originally 20 acres, Rock Island Botanical Preserve is now 120 acres to explore. Mid-summer boasted several vibrant colors and blooms, and the seasonal oak trees are sure to delight in the fall.

There is a diverse range of habitats at Rock Island: wetland, sand prairie, oak savanna, and woodland.

There is a small parking lot that holds about seven cars.

Months of Operation: Open year-round, from sunrise to sunset.

Trails: There is about a half mile of mowed turf trail that I'd consider easy in difficulty.

Bathroom Situation: There are no restrooms at Rock Island Botanical Preserve.

Must See or Do: Practice identifying plants, bring paint sample cards and find matches for each color you brought, keep an eye out for Blanding's or Ornate Box Turtles.

NOTES:

Date Visited:	
Special Memory:	
Something We'd Like to Do Next Time:	

NATURAL AREAS

MATSELL BRIDGE NATURAL AREA

LIST OF ALL OTHERS

MATSELL BRIDGE NATURAL AREA

3742 Matsell Park Road Central City, IA 52214
https://www.linncountyiowa.gov/1021/Matsell-Bridge-
Natural-Area

If you're looking for a place off the beaten path, with unique features and amenities, Matsell Bridge Natural Area is the place for you! The largest natural area in Linn County, this 1,912-acres of land is a treat to explore. My husband and I first visited Matsell while undecided about what to do on a date night. We ended up having a great time walking along the Wapsi River and rescuing freshwater mussels from retreating tributaries.

We were also pleasantly surprised to find a huge, wild sunflower field off the mowed grass trail.

Matsell Bridge Natural Area has hiking, water access with a boat ramp, hunting, equestrian camping and equine trails, a shooting range, an historic ice house from the 1850s, and so much more.

Months of Operation: Open year-round, 4:00 AM-10:30 PM. It should be noted that the equestrian trails are closed to horse riding during the firearm deer hunting season in December.

Pet Information: Dogs must be leashed in all areas of this natural area. There is an equestrian campground as well as many miles of equine friendly trails. Be mindful of hunting season when bringing your pets to Matsell Bridge Natural Area.

Playground: There is no playground.

Lodging: There's a variety of overnight options here at Matsell. There are two pack-in campsites, a main campground, and an equestrian campground. Check the reservation website before choosing your campsite; some are adjacent to parking lots and others have to be hiked-in.

Matsell Bridge also has Linn County's only year-round cabin rental, Red Oak Cabin. This cabin is without electricity or water and is located on a river bluff.

Trails: There are over twelve miles of multi-use trails. They are enjoyed by hikers, horseback riders, bikers, and cross-country skiers. They are primarily mowed grass.

Stroller/ Accessibility: The trails are primarily mowed grass, and not stroller friendly.

Bathroom Situation: There are six restrooms scattered along the natural area. Half of these restrooms are near the Ice House and shooting range.

Other features: The shooting range is a popular spot in Linn County. There is a permit required, which can be purchased on-site on a daily basis. Only paper targets are allowed. This range is closed in January and February each year.

Must See or Do: Find the wild sunflowers in August, keep an eye out for quail, save a mussel or two if the water levels are low.

Spend the night at Red Oak Cabin and remember to appreciate modern amenities when you get back home.

NOTES:

Date Visited:	
Special Memory:	
Something We'd Like to Do Next Time:	

ALL OTHER NATURAL AREAS OF LINN COUNTY

Name: Bird Preserve
Address: 5601 Ellis Blvd., Cedar Rapids
Acres: 140
Hunting: Archery-only deer hunting
Trail: Yes, a grass path
Restrooms: Yes, vault toilets

Name: Blue Creek
Address: 4823 Blue Creek Road, Center Point
Acres: 70
Hunting: All hunting except deer (per donor's request)
Trail: Yes, a grass path. No access allowed during shotgun deer season
Restrooms: No

Name: Buffalo Creek
Address: Linn-Delaware Road, Coggon
Acres: 89
Hunting: Yes- hunting and trapping
Trail: No
Restrooms: No

Name: Chain Lakes
Address: 4247 Chain Bridge Road, Palo
Acres: 491
Hunting: Yes
Trail: Mowed grass in some areas
Restrooms: No

Name: Goose Pond
Address: 3875 Lewis Bottoms Road, Shellsburg
Acres: 269
Hunting: Yes (popular for duck hunting)
Trail: Yes, grass paths
Restrooms: No

Name: Harold and Ruth Rehrauer
Address: 1299 Red Bridge Road, Central City
Acres: 80
Hunting: Yes- hunting and trapping
Trail: Mowed trail
Restrooms: No

Name: Linn Learning Farm
Address: 3 miles north of Palo, west at corner of Hallenbeck and Power Plant Road
Acres: 282
Hunting: Yes- hunting and trapping
Trail: None at this time
Restrooms: No

Name: Lisbon Wildlife Area
Address: West of Lisbon Blvd.
Acres: 92
Hunting: None specified at this time
Trail: No
Restrooms: No

Name: North Cedar
Address: 3410 Cedar Heights Trail, Center Point
Acres: 66
Hunting: None permitted (wildlife refuge)
Trail: Yes, grass paths
Restrooms: No

Name: Otter Creek
Address: 7500 Elf Lane, Cedar Rapids
Acres: 37
Hunting: Bow hunting only (during appropriate season)
Trail: Minimal
Restrooms: No

Name: Palo Marsh
Address: 2935 Palo Marsh Road, Palo
Acres: 144
Hunting: Yes
Trail: Yes, grass paths
Restrooms: No

Name: Paris Bridge
Address: 5301 Sutton Road, Central City
Acres: 83
Hunting: Bow hunting only (during appropriate season)
Trail: No
Restrooms: No

Name: South Cedar
Address: 48 Cedar Park Road, Mount Vernon
Acres: 162
Hunting: Yes
Trail: No
Restrooms: No

Name: Troy Mills
Address: 3200 Coggon Road, Coggon
Acres: 10
Hunting: No
Trail: No, but provides river access for a six hour float to
Central City

Restrooms: No

Name: Wakpicada
Address: Located just south of Central City, adjacent to the Linn County Fairgrounds
Acres: 352
Hunting: Yes
Trail: Yes
Restrooms: Yes- vault toilets

Name: Wickiup Hill (not the learning center)
Address: Two locations- West end of Wickiup Hill Road, and also Green Groves Road in Center Point (between 4066 and 4100)
Acres: 362 at Wickiup Hill Road, 152 at Green Groves Road
Hunting: Yes
Trail: Grass paths at Wickiup Hill Road location, partial grass paths at Green Groves Road
Restrooms: None at either location

BONUS PLACES WORTH EXPLORING

WICKIUP HILL LEARNING CENTER

INDIAN CREEK NATURE CENTER

PRAIRIEWOODS FRANCISCAN SPIRITUALITY CENTER

LOWE PARK

MOUNT TRASHMORE

BEVER PARK

SEMINOLE VALLEY PARK

WICKIUP HILL LEARNING CENTER

10260 Morris Hills Road Toddville, IA 52341
https://www.linncountyiowa.gov/1671/Wickiup-Hill-Learning-Center

Wickiup Hill Learning Center is the epicenter of natural world learning for all ages in Linn County. Wickiup has an indoor learning space, many desirable and well-maintained trails, and the inspired Wandering Woods natural playground.

Aside from the amenities, Wickiup also hosts several learning opportunities and events for children and adults alike. I recommend you check their website regularly for upcoming programming, much of which is free is low cost.

Months of Operation: Year-round, outdoor areas are open from sunrise to sunset. See below for learning center hours:
Monday - Friday 8:00 AM-4:00 PM
Saturday 10:00 AM-4:00 PM
Sunday 1:00-4:00 PM (April through October)

Pet Information: Pets are allowed in outdoor areas, but must be leashed at all times.

Playground: The Wandering Woods playground is a dream! It has ample opportunities for imaginative and creative play, and is fun for all ages. Kids can zipline, climb large structures, build, play music, and use an old fashioned water spigot as they wish. It's definitely one of my favorite playgrounds in the county.

Lodging: There is a replica Wickiup you can reserve for primitive camping.

Trails: There are wetland boardwalks, oak savanna, and prairie woodland trails for walking. The interpretative trail has a storybook walk (occasionally) that kids will enjoy.

Stroller/ Accessibility: The learning center is stroller and wheelchair friendly, as well as the wetland boardwalk. The oak savanna trail is bumpy mowed grass, but I have been able to use a stroller on it in the past.

Bathroom Situation: There are several restrooms inside the learning center, and a non-modern restroom near the primitive campsite.

Other features: Observation deck, bird watching areas, natural habitats and exhibits, naturalists on-site.

Must See or Do: Attend a community event, volunteer with the bird banders, take a short nap in a swinging hammock.

NOTES:

Date Visited:	
Special Memory:	
Something We'd Like to Do Next Time:	

INDIAN CREEK NATURE CENTER

5300 Otis Road SE Cedar Rapids, Iowa 52403
https://indiancreeknaturecenter.org/

The first time we visited Indian Creek Nature Center, I immediately knew that this would be a place we'd return to time and time again. And throughout all four seasons of the year, it has remained a valuable place to connect with nature, play, learn, and meet like-minded people. Indian Creek Nature Center is located off Highway 13 in Cedar Rapids. For over fifty years, the 200 acres of this preserve have served as a place known for developing "champions of nature."

Your family can hike prairie, woodland, or wetland trails any time of the year. Kids will also enjoy the Hazelnut Hideaway natural playground, and all ages can become inspired by the Amazing Space Building, one of the most sustainable buildings in the world. What makes Indian Creek Nature Center stand out, in my opinion, is the amazing variety of events and special programming they host throughout the year.

Months of Operation: Trails are open 365 days a year, from 5:00 AM-10:00 PM.

Amazing Space (the campus and indoor learning center) is open 10:00-4:00 every day from March to October. Amazing Space is closed on Mondays from November to February.

Pet Information: Dogs are allowed on trails but must be leashed. Horses are not permitted, but horseback riding is allowed on the adjacent Sac and Fox Trail maintained by Cedar Rapids Parks Department.

Playground: Hazelnut Hideaway is a fantastic natural playground located right next to Amazing Space. It has several willow branch and stick shelters, a building area, music space, and mud kitchens. Kids can seriously spend hours having open-ended imaginative play here, all within view of a pond and woodland trees. More than once we've found a deer or groundhog checking out the playground as we have arrived!

Lodging: There are no overnight options here, but Amazing Space is available to reserve for weddings, birthday parties, or other private events. If you have a birthday party at Amazing Space, you can select different themes that are carried out by staff naturalists. Our boys and their friends were able to meet many animals up close at their party.

Trails: There are nine different trails at Indian Creek Nature Center, if you include the Cedar Rapids Sac and Fox Trail that leads into the preserve. There are a variety of surfaces and levels of difficulty within these trails. The Wood Duck Way Trail has a boardwalk surface for part of its 1.2 mile loop. When there are more than five inches of snow on the ground, snowshoes are available to rent while walking the trails.

Stroller/ Accessibility: Most trails are stroller friendly, though I would not recommend a stroller on the Cedar Overlook or Woodland Trails (too steep). The prairie trails should be wide enough and maintained well enough for wheelchair use.

Bathroom Situation: There are restrooms inside Amazing Space, but nothing else would be available if the center is closed.

Other features: Creekside Forest Preschool is located at Indian Creek Nature Center, where the next generation of nature enthusiasts get to learn and connect outside.

Down Otis Road is the Penningroth Barn, also owned by ICNC. Not only is the barn area sometimes used for bird banding (which the public is invited to participate in), there is also the Maple Sugar House, where maple syrup is made on-site.

Must See or Do: Check the events calendar for the next festival or guided hike on schedule, attend a free outdoor yoga class during the summer, buy some delicious maple syrup.

NOTES:

Date Visited:	
Special Memory:	
Something We'd Like to Do Next Time:	

PRAIRIEWOODS FRANCISCAN SPIRITUALITY CENTER

120 Boyson Road Hiawatha, IA 52233
https://prairiewoods.org/

Prairiewoods Franciscan Spirituality Center is a place we had previously assumed was not meant for children. Boy, were we wrong! This space is a delight for all ages. Tucked right off of Boyson Road in Hiawatha, Prairiewoods is 70 acres of woods and prairie. There are trails, a labyrinth, gardens, many places to reflect, and a food forest. They've also made strides to create a natural playscape for kids.

Prairiewoods also hosts several unique and fulfilling events and programs throughout the year. They offer yoga, art classes, meditation, overnight retreats, and so much more. Our family enjoys walking the prairie area and nibbling on delicious fruit found in the food forest.

Months of Operation: Year-round. The Center, their main building, is open Monday-Friday 8:00 AM-5:00 PM, as well as select weekends.

Pet Information: Leashed pets welcome.

Playground: While there is no playground, there is a natural playscape and labyrinth.

Lodging: There is a guest house and two hermitages available for reservations. The guest house operates a bit like a bed and breakfast, with several rooms available for guests to choose from. You can also buy a day pass for the guest house. The hermitages are small cottages available for a two-night minimum stay.

Trails: There are two and a half miles of walking trails that connect to various key points of Prairiewoods. You can also take a cosmic walk behind the Center.

Stroller/ Accessibility: This place is stroller and wheelchair friendly, and the main floor of the guest house is accessible.

Bathroom Situation: There are restrooms inside a few of the buildings.

Other features: There are also thirty plots for a community garden and several spots designed to offer moments of peace and reflection. Inside the Center you can find a gift shop, media center, and meditation room.

Must See or Do: Join a drum circle, take a walk through the prairie, meditate in Founders Grove near the Willow, pluck a plum from the Four Winds Food Forest.

NOTES:

Date Visited:	
Special Memory:	
Something We'd Like to Do Next Time:	

LOWE PARK

4500 N 10th Street Marion, IA 52302
https://www.cityofmarion.org/recreation/parks-recreation/facilities/arts-environment-center

Lowe Park pretty much has it all: an arts center, amphitheater, playground, trails, pond, community garden plots, a Master Gardener Greenhouse and demonstration garden, baseball diamond, and a cricket field. It's the gem of Marion!

This park reminds me of the 'glamping' version of outdoor leisure; it's a way to enjoy nature while still having plenty of amenities at hand. The trails are well paved, the land is consistently kept and clean, and the landscape details are gorgeous. In addition to its cleanliness and vast prairie, there are several sculptures and art pieces to observe throughout the park.

Months of Operation: Park is open year-round. The Arts and Environment Center is only open on weekdays 7:00 AM-4:00 PM.

Pet Information: Pets allowed outside, must be leashed. Dogs are not permitted on the playground equipment, and are discouraged from being present in the baseball diamond area.

Playground: A fantastic all-inclusive playground was built in 2019. It's geared for ages 5-12, but I've noticed much younger (and older) kids enjoying the equipment. The playground has its own parking lot off the Irish Drive entrance.

Lodging: There are no overnight options, but several options for event reservations. Patrons can reserve different rooms in the Arts and Environment Center; these range in size and cost. The playground also has an open air shelter available for reservations.

Trails: There are several recreational trails that connect to one another and loop around Lowe park, as well as a sculpture trail that is pleasing to the eye. The sculpture trail is located near the 10th Street entrance.

Stroller/ Accessibility: All trails are stroller and wheelchair accessible.

Bathroom Situation: There are restrooms inside the Arts and Environment Center, as well as a seasonable restroom near the inclusive playground. There are portable restrooms near the baseball diamonds and cricket field.

Other features: Lowe Park hosts several fun (and free) community events, including: concerts, fireworks shows, a kite festival, and an international festival.

Must See or Do: Go fishing for bluegills in the pond, attend a free concert in the park, scope out the community garden plots for inspiration.

NOTES:

Date Visited:	
Special Memory:	
Something We'd Like to Do Next Time:	

MOUNT TRASHMORE

2250 A Street SW Cedar Rapids, Iowa 52404
https://www.solidwasteagency.org/mount-trashmore

Talk about turning trash into treasure! Mount Trashmore is a former landfill site located near Newbo and Czech Village in Cedar Rapids. Six million tons of trash have transformed into a local and tourist destination hot spot. Walk or bike using one of the trails to the top of the mount and you'll be rewarded with an unbeatable scenic overlook of the city.

When you arrive at Mount Trashmore, you are required to check-in through the recreation building. The recreation building itself has restrooms, hydration stations, bike repair stations, and picnic tables.

I'd be remiss if I didn't note that on the day we walked to the top of Mount Trashmore, we found several ticks on us and our dog. This will of course depend on the year; wear protective gear and pack spray just in case.

Months of Operation: Mount Trashmore is seasonal. Depending on weather conditions, it's generally open from April-early November.

Pet Information: Pets allowed and must be leashed.

Playground: There is no playground on Mount Trashmore.

Lodging: There are no lodges or pavilions available.

Trails: There are three recreational trails: Stumptown, Trashmore, and Overlook. Stumpdown Trail does not allow bikes or strollers, and is the longest trail at one mile (5,000 feet elevation gain). Stumptown has some steep grades. Trashmore is a downhill-only trail and only for bikes. Two inch or wider tires are recommended. Overlook Trail is the best bet for multi-age families. It's the easiest, and allows walking, bikes, and strollers. It should be noted that you are not allowed to go off-trail anywhere at Mount Trashmore.

Stroller/ Accessibility: We were able to use a stroller on the Overlook Trail. There are also ADA compliant parking spots and permission to drive to the top if you have a handicap placard.

Bathroom Situation: There are restrooms inside the recreation building.

Other features: There is also a gathering space inside the building, and an overall friendly atmosphere that encourages walkers and bikers to hang out and socialize.

Must See or Do: Try the Trashmore challenge! Check on website for more details.

NOTES:

Date Visited:	
Special Memory:	
Something We'd Like to Do Next Time:	

BEVER PARK

2700 Bever Ave SE Cedar Rapids, IA 52403
https://www.cedar-rapids.org/residents/
parks_and_recreation/parks.php

Bever Park has a wide range of amenities and activities for families to enjoy! With almost 92 acres of land in the heart of historic Cedar Rapids, Bever is a real treat to the community. Whether your family enjoys taking a walk, visiting with farm animals, playing on playgrounds, or swimming in a city pool, there's a little something for everyone.

Old MacDonald's Farm truly sets Bever Park apart from anywhere else in the area. We love to take the kids here in the early summer to meet the new baby animals. The staff and volunteers who work at the farm are extremely helpful and knowledgeable.

Months of Operation: Park is open year round, from 6:00 AM-10:00 PM.

Pet Information: Dogs allowed on leash. Note: dogs not permitted in or near Old MacDonald's Farm.

Playground: Yes, there are a few different playgrounds grouped together at the entrance of the park. They've been recently updated and cater to a wide range of ages.

Lodging: There are four pavilions available to rent at Bever Park: Bever, Grandview, Red Oak, and Zoo Hill. Prices range from $84-$163. There are several picnic table areas available on a first come, first served basis.

Trails: There is an easy, short trail at Bever. It's about half a mile, with limited elevation gain.

Stroller/ Accessibility: Most of the park has sidewalks or paved roads for strollers or wheelchair accessibility. The sidewalk has a ramp.

Bathroom Situation: There is one permanent restroom.

Other features: Something truly unique to Bever Park is Old MacDonald's Farm. An important part of the city for over one hundred years, Old MacDonald's is a free petting farm open to the public from May to October (exact dates vary each year). Donations of at least one dollar per person recommended. Kids of all ages will love getting to encounter pigs, cows, goats, and more up close. You can also feed the animals.

Another cool feature of Bever Park is its outdoor pool. Open during the summer months, Bever Pool has swim lanes, free swim areas, and water slides. You must pay to use this pool.

Must See or Do: Visit the baby farm animals when it first opens for the season (before they get too big and ornery), pick an apple from one of the apple trees, and do a cannonball in the pool.

NOTES:

Date Visited:	
Special Memory:	
Something We'd Like to Do Next Time:	

SEMINOLE VALLEY PARK

5925 Seminole Valley Trail Cedar Rapids, IA 52411
http://crgis.cedar-rapids.org/ParksFinder/default.htm;
http://www.seminolevalleyfarmmuseum.net/

What Seminole Valley Park lacks in playground equipment it makes up for in natural beauty. Nestled between the Cedar River and Ushers Ferry Historic Village, Seminole Valley is 202 acres. This park features an old airplane statue that the kids will get a kick out of, a farm museum, cricket courts, a cross-country course (popular for local school competitions), and a cross-country ski course for the winter.

There are many events that take place at the Seminole Valley Farm Museum, including (but not limited to): open air markets, Reflections of the Civil War, and World War II Remembrances. Check out their website for more information: http://www.seminolevalleyfarmmuseum.net/

Months of Operation: Park is open year round, from 6:00 AM-10:00 PM. The gates are closed to motor vehicles in the winter, so you need to park on the street near the entrance. It's not a far walk.

Pet Information: Dogs allowed on leash.

Playground: There isn't a playground at Seminole Valley.

Lodging: There is one pavilion available for reservation, Valley View, for $84. It is located near the cricket court.

Trails: The Seminole Valley Trail is a 2.4 mile loop on a combination of gravel and dirt. The trail hugs the Cedar River and features a woodland area. About 75% into the trail, however, the trail narrows almost impossibly thin and is hard to locate. I had to follow bike tread marks to find my way back to the entrance of the park. There are also cross-country 4K, 5K, 6K, and 8K routes. Maps for those courses can be found on the Cedar Rapids Parks and Recreation website. In the winter, there is a two-mile cross-country ski trail near the entrance of the park.

Stroller/ Accessibility: Strollers and wheelchairs can use the sidewalk path with ease, but in regards to the loop trail, it would only be accessible until the gravel ends. From there, the trail is too narrow, bumpy, and covered with logs to access.

Bathroom Situation: There are two permanent restrooms at Seminole Valley.

Other features: Some unique features of Seminole Valley Park include: Farm Museum, cricket courts, cross-country courses, and a vintage airplane statue.

Must See or Do: Take your kites and RC toys to the open fields, walk near the river, challenge friends to a cricket match.

NOTES:

Date Visited:	
Special Memory:	
Something We'd Like to Do Next Time:	

WINTER BUCKET LIST

Go searching for frost in the morning

Go sledding at Pinicon Ridge

Rent snowshoes at Indian Creek Nature Center

Look for Bald Eagles while walking the Prairie Park Fishery Loop

Enjoy the areas that are usually the buggiest in the summer

Safely cross a frozen lake (ice should be at least four inches thick)

Go ice fishing

ID animal tracks in the snow while on a hike

Take a hot cocoa walk

Go shed hunting (look for deer antlers that have been shed)

SPRING BUCKET LIST

Try to find skunk cabbage

Play in the mud

Check for 'signs of life'

Find the perfect walking stick

Join the bird banders at Wickiup or Indian Creek Nature Center

Use free paint samples to color match what you find

Press flowers between the pages of a heavy book

Check for peak migration weeks and bird watch

Walk to the top of Mount Trashmore (before it gets too hot)

Take a wildflower walk at J. Harold Ennis Preserve

SUMMER BUCKET LIST

Go camping

Enjoy a beach day at Pleasant Creek

Celebrate Pollinator Week

Go creek stomping at Wapsipinicon State Park

Catch a crayfish

Go paddleboarding, kayaking, or pedal boating at Pinicon Ridge

Go fishing near Waldo's Rock off the Grant Wood Trail

Forage berries, or practice identifying fruiting plants

Check out the food forest at Prairiewoods

Find the wild sunflowers at the Matsell Bridge Natural Area

FALL BUCKET LIST

Volunteer to harvest native seeds

Make elderberry syrup or sumac lemonade

Stay in a cabin

Climb the observation tower at Pinicon Ridge at peak leaf week

Make a stick shelter at Palisades-Kepler

Visit the playground at Morgan Creek

Make confetti with fallen leaves

Enjoy the fall festival at Wickiup Hill Learning Center

Go on a full moon night hike

Forage for mushrooms, or practice identifying fungi

SPECIFIC RECOMMENDATIONS

IF YOU'RE LOOKING FOR _____________, GO TO _____________.

Indoor Learning Centers	Indian Creek Nature Center or Wickiup Hill Learning Center
Creek Stomping	Wapsipinicon State Park, Morgan Creek, or Indian Creek Nature Center
A Day at the Beach	Pleasant Creek State Park
Doggie Fun	Wanatee, Pinicon Ridge, or the Dave Wright Family Dog Park (near Cedar Valley Nature Trail)
Fall Leaf Peeping	Palisades-Kepler or observation tower at Pinicon Ridge
Sledding	Wanatee Park or Pinicon Ridge
Fishing	Matsell Bridge Natural Area or Pleasant Creek State Park
Hunting	Natural areas (check for specific guidelines in natural areas chapter)
Free Outdoor Yoga	Lowe Park or Indian Creek Nature Center
Cave Exploring	Wapsipinicon State Park
Mountain Bike Trails	Wanatee Park, Sac and Fox Trail, Beverly Park, Creek Confluence at Boyson Trail
Cross-Country Ski Trails	Wickiup, Matsell Bridge, Wanatee, Morgan Creek

ADDITIONAL RESOURCES

Books:

1. *Balanced and Barefoot: How Unrestricted Outdoor Play Makes for Strong, Confident, and Capable Children* by Angela Hanscom
2. *1000 Hours Outside Activity Book* by Ginny Yurich
3. *The Doorstep Mile* by Alastair Humphreys
4. *Outdoor Kids in an Inside World: Getting Your Family Out of the House and Radically Engaged with Nature* by Steven Rinella
5. *Newcomb's Wildflower Guide* by Lawrence Newcomb

Websites:

1. Iowa Department of Natural Resources (DNR): https://www.iowadnr.gov/
2. Cedar Rapids Parks and Recreation: https://www.cedar-rapids.org/residents/parks_and_recreation/index.php
3. Cedar Rapids Parks Finder: http://crgis.cedar-rapids.org/ParksFinder/default.htm
4. Cedar Rapids Tourism: https://www.tourismcedarrapids.com/
5. Linn County Conservation: https://www.linncountyiowa.gov/conservation
6. Linn County Trails Association: https://linncountytrails.org/
7. Trail Link: https://www.traillink.com/
8. Outgrown (formerly Hike it Baby): https://weareoutgrown.org/

9. Linn Area Mountain Bike Association: https://www.linnareamtb.org/
10. Women's Mountain Bike Group: https://www.fearlesswomenofdirt.com/

Apps:

1. Iowa State Park Passport
2. iNaturalist
3. Merlin Bird ID
4. 1000 hours outside tracker
5. Geocaching
6. orienteer.co

ENJOYING NATURE AS AN ADULT

Spending time in nature isn't just beneficial for children. Some might argue it's even more important for adults to get outside. So you're not a hiker? That's okay! There are plenty of other ways to be outside; I encourage you to find what makes being outdoors the most fun and revitalizing. Here is a short list of ideas:

- Hiking
- Foraging
- Orienteering (use the app listed under resources for local challenges!)
- Water Activities: swimming, paddleboarding, kayaking, skiing
- Snow Activities: cross-country skiing, snow shoeing, making a snowman or having a snowball fight
- Biking
- Fishing
- Hunting
- Yoga or meditation
- Tapping into inner child discovery and play
- Cosplay or LARPing
- Reading
- Sketching or collecting (allowable) artifacts for crafting
- Bird watching
- Practicing plant, fungi, or insect identification using iNaturalist app
- Volunteering
- Pulling invasive plant species from natural areas
- Early morning or late night walks

ACKNOWLEDGEMENTS

This book is the culmination of many hands and minds from this beloved community. First, a big thank you to my family for joining me on so many fun outings (or, 'field research'). Ryan, these outdoor trips are some of my favorite family memories. Cal and Ben, even if it sometimes required a 'sweet treat' to get you on the trails, I don't regret a single bribe. In you two boys we find the best adventures.

A heap of gratitude to the rangers and staff at both the state and county level. The kind people at the Iowa DNR and Linn County Conservation Department handled my numerous calls and emails about property lines and accessibility with patience and expertise. Specifically, thank you to the following folks: Meredith Glynn, Shaun Reilly, Jason Baumann, Aaron Batchelder, Julie Tack, Lucas Wagner, and Matt Bonar.

I'm grateful for the Cedar Rapids branch of Hike it Baby, and all the great parents and kids who we get to wander around with on Monday mornings. To Ashley, thank you for being the first reader of this book. Laura, thank you for the valuable information about LAMBA and orienteering. I appreciate both of you for sharing an enthusiasm about nature (especially skunk cabbage!).

A big thank you to my friend Annalise Santillan for this gorgeous cover and artful photos. I'd like to thank Audrey White for telling me about the 1000 Hours Outside Challenge, and Ginny Yurich for creating it. And lastly, to the families of Linn County, thank you for investing in this book and your family's precious time outside in nature. I wrote this for you.

Author photo by Sarah Fridono

ABOUT THE AUTHOR

Brianna is a mother, naturalist, writer, and educator. When she isn't attempting to take fancy pictures of fungus, she's likely wrestling with her two boys or trying to take a nap.

You can follow Brianna on Instagram @moments.in.nature.ia, or check out her website at acceptingagape.com